HYPERBOLE

T0359604

By the same author:

The Things the Mind Sees Happen (chapbook), 2019

HYPERBOLE

BELINDA RULE

RECENT
WORK
PRESS

Hyperbole
Recent Work Press
Canberra, Australia

Copyright © Belinda Rule, 2021

ISBN: 9780645009033 (paperback)

 A catalogue record for this
book is available from the
National Library of Australia

All rights reserved. This book is copyright. Except for private study,
research, criticism or reviews as permitted under the Copyright Act,
no part of this book may be reproduced, stored in a retrieval system, or
transmitted in any form by any means without prior written permission.
Enquiries should be addressed to the publisher.

Cover image: 'Le Soleil' by Thomas Bresson. Reproduced under
Creative Commons Attribution 2.0
Cover design: Recent Work Press
Set by Recent Work Press

recentworkpress.com

SS

Contents

i

Poem of a new driver

When I first get the car, I pull all the fabric
of the city towards me, race it through
like cloth beneath the presser foot.
Come here, Geelong! And it does:
a bolt of satin sky unrolls,
the road a seatbelt
speeding on its reel.

You see so much of the sky driving:
you're an eel darting upwards
in a bright bowl of glass,
trailing the road like a tail.
            So much of trees, too,
distilled by speed. When you walk
there is only one tree,
and your beetling body labouring below.

And always you know you might die.
A second's distraction, and
you will swerve, careen, flip,
and in mid-air, you will be
the master of something new,
a mote exploding from the sun,
the knower of what
            may only be known once,
                        and then only for a second,
at last,
            purely happy.

Exile

A calf had slipped the loose-strung wire,
and the herd in committee milled close
as if to reabsorb him, a mercury drop.
Small, dark, tufted boy,
eyes like clean leadlights.
He stared, the bald, fearing,
hating way a child of eight will stare
at a stranger, careless of offense.

Always you think a cow is about to
speak, give up the pretence of
thick-tongued chewing, of middle-distanced eye,
and focus—the way an acquaintance
at a bus stop will blink and suddenly
        see you—and utter
something. As if you met a wild woman,
come down from a long stay upon
a wooded hill—hair grown brush-thick to the waist,
dirt laid on the grease of the skin
till it burnished to permanence
—still you would look in her strange eye and see
knowledge, and you could have words,
the meeting of knowing-speaking minds.

Thinking to help, I took a step.
A great mother cow
stretched her tufted neck
        and screamed,
curdling, sound like metal
torn from metal, the others joining
as if burning alive. A whole room of people
refusing to know me, like some
dream.

The slow clock

In a gully we found it: hash of fallen trunks
like the ribs of a great beast. But
we were too old for it, too big to squeeze within
and too prissy, afraid of the doings of ants
and unknown others, intricate civilisations
and workings of rot, the dried bark half-way back
to dirt, and some maze, some great working
beneath the surface.

Up on Bald Hill, the grey shrubs grew knee-high,
slanted to the salt wind, flowered sometimes
purple like dusk, ochre like sand,
testament to endless endurance, endurance
without goal, without hope.
By night, if you left the track and sat,
shrub-high, you could simply be
gone.

The dull-scaled goanna,
shrunken in its hide as if the flesh
had perished since some past
moist plenitude,
moved in stop-motion, cranking
the cogs of its shoulders. We hung the rubbish
out of reach, beat spades on the ground,
while it licked the air like a slow clock.
Did it leave, whale swimming the dust,
for fear of us, or on its own prerogative?

Everything was wrong with me,
the purple welts where the unsought
woman-body erupted, faster than the skin could stretch,
the fat like off-casts of food.
It was wrong with her too,

and I made a model of her fat rolls in the sand
for her to find. She tore apart my *B*-shaped pen,
threw the plastic in the dirt to warp and fade.
In the tent she rolled on me, savage even
when she'd left her body in sleep, pressed my face
in the stinking mildewed cloth, her on top of me
and her bedding on top of us both.

Each day the sun came up in the tent fly.
A sheet of light on the estuary,
flies rising from the trees like steam.
Each day the lighting of the stove,
one flame for each family.

Age of reason

In a bank on a weekday,
I saw a younger girl,
blonde hair in pink clips,
spiral glitter sneaker laces
        —baubles of a treasured child
that no-one ever bought for me.
A girl in a parlour painting,
and I the hairy spider
hulking in the corner of the frame.

In the war-room of the mind,
I pierced my map with pins. How simple
to trick her to some dirty culvert,
hold her down, mar her white arms,
beat, mutilate, throttle,
kill her. The thing would be
to borrow some of my father's tools—
perhaps that hammer, that handsaw, that small chisel
whose edge shone from sharpening.
I was larger than her, stronger,
and had the key to the crankshaft
of the well of the world's evil,
secret prize surely slipped me
for merit.

I only swung on the queue ropes
then left with my mother,
but I could see how easily
it could have gone otherwise.
The world of banks, of mothers with shopping,
of cars humming peaceably in lanes,
was at any time a single breath away
from savagery, fire, riot in the street.
Civilisation was a hair draped

on the head of a pin, each one of us
        poised, rigid,
clutching our own pin still—I could see
I would cramp with the effort
all my life.

Gospel

You don't need to tell me how
Daniel always wins, for I
am the difference between
two pieces of cake. Later I will find him
and exact my reward—the strawberry
sliding down my gullet and
onto the floor. I have no gullet.

I am the thing that falls off the shelf
when nothing has fallen.
I am the ringing in your ears.

I come from where you go
when you don't appear to be here. On windy nights,
I pop the thumbtacks out of the wall.

If you
stare down the barrel
of your empty pupil,
you will not find me.
Beneath the spongy green rim
of your iris, I curl up to
stay still, which is
sleep.
          Other times,
I inhabit the space between
the dust and the floor, where
I see what no-one else has seen
or will see: the shadows of the dust,
small as seeds of snowflakes.

Before I was here,
I was there,
        and I said to them,

You will not stop seeking until you find,
and when you find, you will be disturbed,
and when you are disturbed, you will probably
spill something and
stain your shirt.

I said to them,
Lift up a stone,
find a spider, fat as a grape.
Do not split a piece of wood,
or I do not know what
I will be tempted to do.

I say to you now,
I have cast fire upon letters
left too close to candles, I have
stolen mustard seeds to cast
at rocks, the space between
the lid and the jar
ticklish around my middle.
I have parted the very walls and
marched the ants through. I say,

Run, and I will be
tucked up in the heel
of your shoe, gnawing at the lining.

Renovations in the suburbs

One night, I was thirteen;
the trees stood over the dark yard
quiet, the way I thought all nights were quiet,
the neighbours, dogs and bicycles
packed away in their boxes, posed for the mould.
The red round clock purse-legged: midnight
and they had not returned.

A secret warranty had expired. Perhaps I should
up-end the vases for rattling keys, ruffle the phone bills.

On the porch, the gutter gushed down a post,
wet leaves like shattered glass
jangling in the dark. Cars
sizzled by—not theirs.

I could crack, hard, open, if I liked,
the dancing gnome of München on his
painted china egg,
whose arse I'd been made wipe
free of dust, spritz
of stasis and subjugation.
And I did like. Their loathed clothes
I would fly as flags in the street.
The sofa I had been kept off
like a dog, let it meet
the scissors I was forbidden to cut with.

They returned at one, found me
presiding at the table,
fist served up on the cloth
like a roast.

Gestalt with seagulls

Late at night, in the rain
I drove to the end of the quay,
past the lights of the refinery,
its single outlet flame
streaming in the wind like a pennant.
Between the hulking dark of the shipbuilders
and a car-park jungle of dillweed
was a wide curved verge, seamless with the road.
It was there that I found them:
the seagulls—the secret
of where they go at night.
Like snowfall on the road,
a tight-hooked rug of white fleece nubs:
no road, no verge, only birds.

I drove at them. The carpet rose, as if shaken out
by a mighty hand, peeled up and off the ground
and dispersed, shredded, in the rain,
just as the impulse that had woken me,
angry, from a dream of my mother, and sent me
to the car, to drive the docks at night
was already gone.

I parked at the edge of the quay,
at the crest of a bluestone wall
holding back the leaping bay.
The light of the city lay in sheets
on the face of the rain. And then,
above the rude
maracas of water on the roof
came the delicate thud and shuffle
of countless seagulls settling on the car.

Highway, Shepparton

Did you know, the other day
I drove that northern road again? Who knew
you could assail the country of childhood
so simply: just get in the car and go.

But this country
was not our country. The road
I sought, long, straight and pale,
lay beneath another road, across a membrane
I could not pierce. Still the ragged lady gums
danced their set across the river bridge,
but the drought had lifted:
the hearts of the horse-tail grass were green,
the paddocks chartreuse, nubbled velvet strewn
with what I took to be litter, but later saw
was a voluminous cast of white cockatoos,
gorging on plenty.

But of course you don't know—
        you are not here to tell.
The membrane is thickening,
and that country is drifting away.
There is no-one here with me
to watch it go

ii

Family photos

The dark half
of my face, in the shade of the tree
could have been anything.
How would you know?

It could have been
all rust and silver trout scales, each
bright as a coin,
sharp as a knife.

It could have been an open wound:
slit fish quivering,
wet as a mangled mouth.

What would you know,
about the cavern in my body,
the groaning of wind,
the grinding of rocks?
How would its song sound
should I pop off the top
and speak?
Like the beating of wings?
The scream of a bird?
          The sound of a phone, bleating
like a rabbit in a trap,
in a house, when you know
the caller is me,
and I am calling to tell you:
this.

Found photo

He has grown a beard
like a wild man, and his hair flies out
like the dandelion fuzz
of boyhood. Beneath a foreign road sign,
burnt face, white eyes, that nose
like a bag stuffed with knuckles.
Desert prophet in a cave—
what have you come
to tell me?

What is love when
absence is perpetual? A plug
ever unsocketed. Some rubbish
thrown from a window at speed.

Won't you come home, my love,
I have only destroyed everything
you ever knew, knocked down the house
and razed the land, changed my name, and
cut off my face and burnt it. Aside from that
I am the same.

Mum

Suddenly, in the glass, facet-edged,
an enemy. My hand,
twined trembling in the tap's calyx,
is a drunk's hand, deep
flutter of wine along sinew,
and idiotic, I am granted prophecy,
that approach to the still waters
permitted only those
dumb as a filled urn.

Crowned awkward with feathers of maidenhair,
I see: my crumpled iris-rim lip
            is her lip;
the fine spoked wheel beneath my grimacing eye
has etched itself deep with years on her face.
The wet red meat of my viscera is made of her,
a shy-hood I cannot take off,
the text that writes my living flesh
bad at the source.

Letters home

What about this, then: I letterbox everyone
we have ever known, and we all stage you a play
of The Frog and the Scorpion.
Your friend the potter, who now can't be mine,
could make us a gilt-fired tail,
too lovely to break. One of the children
should be the one to ride the frog. The frog
should be a strong swimmer, at least
at first.

What about this: God descends, says, Fine,
I am stopping the earth
till I can make you understand.
Cars, bins, dogs, people
would drift off into space, the atmosphere
disperse to the void. Look at that cow
explode across the remains of the sky.
You amaze me
again.

Mum, again

Somewhere out in the world you are
aging, shrinking in on yourself,
a little brown leaf. Only a little
of what will happen in time
has yet happened
but still, you are the age your father was
when he died, angry,
paper-faced and rotting inside.
I hear of you only second-hand now,
and most of what I hear
is that you speak ill of me, which is
an injury softened by use and accustomment
almost to melody: an old song sung
by a voice in a crowd, as I pass on a bicycle.

What I did hear is this:
your tender toes, shoved too young
in high-heeled shoes, have had their day in court
at last. They point now, fixed, at the sky, or perhaps
up at you, accusing. A therapeutic shoe is prescribed,
round-toed, laced-up, institutional.

What wound to your febrile vanity. What torching
of your best, most beloved plans.
This is the birthright I have lost:
to hear you speak of it. To write it in the book of me,
to know it is coming for me too, the wound
to my febrile vanity, the torch to my
most beloved plans. I will go into age
alone, mapless.

Oh, already a faint lithograph print
of the creases on your old woman's face
has settled across my face, a spider's web
in your wicked image.

The difference between the mind and the other

I was kept from my grandmother's body
but I see it white and the pleats of the neck
falling from the ridge of the chin,
bare promontory in a land
where discontent is forever,
where that inhaled breath
            should a child raise its voice
is held forever. The tight wire of curls
at the temples is a judge's wig.
The case for unhappiness heard, the court rules:
            yes.
Court is adjourned, and she retires
to a land, perhaps, beneath a greyish sky,
rimmed by quiet waters. Night falls only
slowly; no light ever bobs
to disturb the dusk.

Now that my mother, though living, is lost to me
I have tried to stop being angry, to put down
my end of the rope.
But the rope keeps tugging back,
worse now I know for sure
there was never anyone
on the other end but me,
me as simulacrum of the other,
made perfect, powerful, indefatigable,
set upon myself with devilish adamance.
It is said all love is projection.
Perhaps it is me upon that island
in the lightless sea.
Elsewhere, the other is dying,
inconsolable, the instruments
of the body unwired, watching

the formed clay of self erode to mud
as if consciousness were nothing, electrical accident,
while I joust with air,
defeat myself.

I am trying to throw things away

Say, these two cups,
his always green, mine always blue,
in the long dark the two of us,
me stacked inside him, or him
stacked inside me.

What even is this—
museum of the artefacts
of people who did not love me
enough? See here, this
teal-handled knife, from a caravan set.
How careless she buttered her bread then,
bikini bottoms ruched like a shower cap,
face cast down in the slide frame, still years away
from fool enough
to imagine a child.

But I wake in the night, afraid I
really did throw those cups away.
Lurch to the kitchen.
They are here. The moon is senseless
on the neighbour's car. I am part
of a chess set and all the other pieces
are misery; I cannot discard them;
they cannot discard me; there is only
gambit and check, gambit and check,
back in the box and start again,
          and what if I just threw
everything from a high place then
ran down and set it alight? I'd have
to buy more, and all I seem to have
in my purse is this one pearl button
and this tie-pin, slightly rusted.

Rooms

All night and day it rains,
till at dusk I lift a window for the air
and my lost brother is outside,
slick with rain, disdaining
the bamboo pergola in his wild way—
leaper into deep pools, eater
of unnecessary chillis.
How handsome he is. How well
age wears his face.
He does not see me.

Now all
the empty rooms of the holiday house
are full of my lost family.
How did I not see they were here?
I can hear the children
I've never met
bouncing on the candlewicked beds
beside their lost parents;
they shriek like whipbirds.
On a dry patch of deck, my lost mother
and the man recline with wine,
tanned, loose, happy.
She slides the flywire, mind on dinner,
and her eye
              slips right through me.

Pants! Notes towards a musical

Too hot in the night
I kicked off my pants, and
unknown to me
they fell down the side of the bed.
Three times I woke from sleep
frantic for pants, tore up the covers
like a mole in a lawn. No pants! I cried
on the moors for pants, love's labour
lost. It was the east and pants
were the sun.

In the daylight I find
a false back in the cupboard does not open
on a hoard of smuggled kittens
I hide from the police, the sweet
hearts of all onions have not been
shy striated worms all along, and it beggars belief that
my indifferent mother would ever
            saw me free from a coconut,
even first having saved the milk to sell.

What is the loss of pants
            but a promise
that pants may be restored?
And with pants, everything. But
the day dawns motherless,
its cupboards bare.

Who made the bird drop

On the occasion of a funeral

Who made the bird drop
into the valley like a stone,
scything the air in halves
sweet as a peach?
Who made the valley fall away
so sharp and sweet, the earth bitten open
avid and deep? Who fluffed the plush
canopy of the trees
and inked the black beneath?

Is this yours: distant thunder of laughter
from the lights behind the glass
as I stand here in the dark, apart?
What about this stone like a sickle,
small as a coin? This leaf like a tongue?
This roaring across the valley that could be
anything. Is that you?

Evening

Even now as the light falls and the cars
are tucked behind the letterboxes
and the sun strobes low between the paperbarks
and a dog bolts for joy across the grass, yellow
like photos of 1983 which is the last time anyone
even pretended to be happy,
even now is there not some driveway I could turn down
where someone is waiting for me.

Men

I only like imaginary
men,
the ones who think
my art is
the most transporting
thing they have ever seen,
and I am exactly as
hilarious as I actually,
actually am.

Even then, even then
not really. Maybe I'd rather
walk off into the dark,
chew the trees, burrow,
make a hat of yellow fireweed
big as a child (that I won't have).
Perhaps in the end
forget my own name,
which might, actually, be
for the best.

Pulled teeth, age 36

How like it was to that other time
I'd been made lie still and
let a man hurt me.
The next day, four deep wells
plugged with clotted blood,
tunnel to an unknowable core, exit
to another world.
And the private, inward face
of the next molar along, seen
for the first time: pale and pleasing,
round as a buttock,
the fangy parts piratical,
jagged as a leaf.

At once I was sorry
I'd declined to take the teeth—
it'd seemed obscene. What knowings
might I have had of them?
Their roots, tuber-like, part
of the iceberg below the water,
mother-of-pearl striations of
cream, beige and bone,
their spit, blood and tartar.
The shape of them like two cocked
lizards' muzzles, scenting
the air of the silent country within, now
breaking its silence for the first and perhaps
last time, to send me this telegram of
        faithful teeth:
near-last friends from middle childhood,
only children I might ever have.

On waking with the pain

Now in the night I wake to it:
plucking of a cello string,
low hoot of wind in a deep cave,
song of wrongness sounding,
          sounding.

The hand is unmarred to look at,
paragon of itself, sweet in sleep
as a small bald mouse
curled in the nest of its mother.
Nothing hurts it. But oh,
          it hurts.
Someone is crying for help
in a locked house; I cannot get in.

In the hallway mirror I see
the slumped back, fattish neck, arm
dangled like a butchered fowl.
What fool left me here
in charge of this body?

All the world put away in its box
but us: the body and I. What to do but sit
and wait, in the mesh-curtained streetlight,
by the grey quiet
          of the television, the shapes
of the dirty glasses.
Sit! Are we not a good dog? The hand
inert in our lap: look what we've fetched. Surely
the master comes back for us
by morning.

The loved body

The loved shoulder of a stranger is an
awkward thing to bear, sweet unbitten
curve of baked-bread skin, sweet unpressed
dough in the fold of the arm. But what good is
anything when I can't fuck, because the self
imagined in the other's eye is impossible,
some golem of broken form, half-dried
in the sun, falling down like a bombed city.
Once as a child I loved me to the point of
lust, stared close at the sand-snake meanders
of the crease inside my elbow. To lick there,
hot and copper-bright, was almost sex.
Now everything belongs to the other, that loved
serene unknowing body, laughing, walking on.

Sex is okay but

Have you driven the Nullarbor,
have you stood on the cliffs at Eucla
and looked down at the Bight, at the
bitten-through cake
of a continent.

Sex is okay but
have you suddenly in mid-life
begun to love your father, have you
fallen on him, stroked his piebald brows,
scrunched like a frogmouth's. Has he frozen
as if in fear, for
it is you who is the frogmouth!
Your predator's beak
so close to his eye.

Sex is okay but
have you had a poem published
in a really famous journal.

Have you flown twenty-six hours London to Melbourne
then lain down in your own bed.

Have you seen your friends do the things
they were always afraid to do—leave,
divorce, come out—
seen them almost get taller,
better dressed, less angry.

Have you fallen in with the neighbour girls
cheers-ing on their porch, who say, at the Yachtie
they've banged every dude there,
have you brought them to a hush
and lured them to confess:

most sex is shit,
and they can't get wet
half the time either.

The end of men

The man on the train
the Maths 142 exam at the Showgrounds.
He had used
a Reject Shop catalogue
to form a little tent.

The man at night at the end of my street—
tall, pale, forties, blue shirt, I told the cops.
No, I did not want a patrol.

The man who made my friend at twelve
change schools.

The time late at night
on the tram 19 to Moreland, last stop before depot.
Hydraulics at the doors. A face, brilliant
smiling to the right. The elbow
          going.
I got off. He was carried away
to the silence of the depot shed.
Always I wondered
what happened next.
Did he jizz all night
alone in the cavernous dark
among the sleeping trams, just jizz
          and jizz?
In the morning when he tried to leave
the gates were locked.
          Men began to fall
from a chute in the ceiling. First
they cried out, breaking bones, but the later
arrivals fell on the earlier, and were cushioned.
Women had had enough, had taken the world
          at last. Only the tram depot

was for men now. We were building dildos
out in the world where we were free,
beautiful glistening pink dildos with no
men attached to them at all;
we had seen enough.

The deep water

On rape

A simple and
calamitous truth is that the spirit does
animate the flesh after all.
Held down, you fight
to the end of your strength
and fail. A light goes out;
the spirit leaves the body.

How long can you really
keep dragging this carcass
around? How long
can a bird struggle in a sack? Even if
          you could take wing
in that fibrous dark,
how would you find your way
          to the shore and
                    out across the deep water?
What is across there, anyway? That air
you can watch leave the body,
when an animal dies—can that
be breathed back in? Or perhaps
there is only the water,
          and you have to keep flying
until you can't anymore. The gift
is that then you can stop.

In the long grass

The hair on my arm was close
in the warm brick of the gaslight,
a landscape seen at a distance
from above. These hairs, tiny,
sprung from dark wells, an animal secret;
a secret of creation,
like how we do not know
how our warm fluids can mix and make things,
that most secret and smug silence of all.

I did not ask for this
chalice of destiny in my body, the indignity
of its polishing
and repolishing itself,
perfecting its threat; my will a moth
bumping useless on the lantern.

I am getting freckled, like my mother.
Next I will rumple,
drawing in like a thing shrunk
slowly in an oven;
like tissue paper used, and carefully reused,
the way things used to be used, and carefully reused,
as though there would only ever be one
of anything. And perhaps for me too will come the day
when I seize the plump arm of a child,
to hold it, to pore over it, to love it
greedily—to have the child squirm away,
sensing what I am, there, crouching in the long grass.

In the gaslight, you found on my body
the fractals of nature: the coil of a sea fossil,
the whorl on the belly of a cat.
My body was a world you had come to live in;

you mapped it with a settler's urgency. All of its names
were grand as the names
of a homeland.

What chaff of me
I may have rubbed off on you,
you have long since washed away.
What is a world when no-one lives in it?
You did not put me to paper.
I am beyond the edge of all maps.

Still, I think you must have carried away
a little of me to your new woman. I imagine her
with another woman. By then my pain
will be an anecdote. I imagine them laughing—
I imagine them stylish, and young, and laughing.
Now I am the moth on the lantern
in truth. If only
the light would go out, I could be free.

Lust

Home-time, on a winter afternoon.
The sky is a marbled field
of turquoise wash and fox fur, and
I am gliding through the world
in my whirring metal egg, in a string
of tinsel lights. The rain falls
in sequins, and I think
is there not some handsome man,
some lithe woman, pink-cheeked,
dashing in a plaid scarf,
I could invite inside my warm cocoon? Imagine
the gratitude. Could I not
ply him with wine, lay her down
on a rug before the fire, as payment.

But of course I never do, because
no-one else is real but me.
Sweet, cushioned yolk of my
omnipotent egg: I am the eye of God, the Spirit
moving over the water. It is
at such times I am closest to death—
why should I not
merge in front of that tanker truck, just
when its light are brightest? I am made
after all, only of light, and air,
and some mischief you might call
by many names,
          some of them rude,
some of them lovely.

The stone

After Peter Porter's 'What I have written I have written'

Is the illness illness
or is the illness truth—
key to the temple, on whose altar lies
       the totem
truer than mother, father, sister,
brother, child; the thing
always missing, now found.

But the mind cannot bear witness
against itself.

Better say it was a stone
I found in my string bag,
snug as a sleeping snake.
Black as a country night, hand-long,
with a waist like an elegant doll's.
I thought of the sparrows I chased as a child
wanting, with something
very like sexual passion,
to hold one enclosed and warm
and twitching in my hand,
       and I bit it.
It tasted of cold, and the doings of fire,
and not some dark, rich resin
I could suck into syrup, and take into myself
as perhaps I had hoped.

I left it in the garden,
beside the husk of a caterpillar.
For a moment, had a feeling
       liquid, like love,
that I ought to take it up again,
wash it, keep it with me always.

In the morning found it,
curled mouse in my sock drawer.
The next day, beneath my pillow.
The next day, in my mouth,
prey in the gullet of a python, just
nuzzling the valve.

The things the mind sees happen

They are stored in a box,
jewelled eggs:

The lover who says I'm sorry, I just
don't want you anymore.
I woke up and the light
had gone out.

The father who, quiet in a chair on the porch,
seen in silhouette against
the tall grass at dusk,
is actually dead,
has been that way since morning.

They lie on a table in a sunny room.
Also on the table, cartoned in sixes,
is everything and -one
you have ever loved or wanted.
There are infinite boxes and
none can be told apart and
every rich yolk is quickening in its shell.

I am driving with my father

I am driving with my father
in a place where green and stony hills
rise like mesa, thin and steep,
like the holes in Swiss cheese inverted.
A narrow road winds up
and down and around.
We have to hurry.
My tires plough the verge:
dirt falls to nothing,
starbursts of mustard-gold.
I am trying too hard not to die, to worry
if my father is angry.
Someone else is in the car:
who?

Now we're in Port Arthur, where Mum and Dad
were once together, still in love.
A ruin of sandstone bricks
on a plateau washing away from within,
holes in the ground beneath
as if we're looking down the barrel of stalactites
from a hole in the roof of a cave.
I am so careful, so slow.

No, it's not Port Arthur, it's College Crescent and
all the students' dormitories
are falling down in the holes in the ground.
I try to drive but all the students
want to talk to me, they have a form
they had to fill out; now no-one
is taking the form, or doing the thing
they need to do with the form.
Everyone is disappointed in me. In the corner
the office has crumbled
to the green abyss.

Where is my father? By the car
by a fallen colonnade, like ancient Rome.
The other person lurks behind a column,
face in shadow. Who is that?

But we need to go: we need to drive
up a mesa thin as a needle in the distance,
ascend a narrow spiral of road
into the clouds, where surely I will miss the turn
and let us fall and die:
I am eager to begin.

The night train

One day you will realise,
though you will not remember
which day, since the days are
in the end much the same,
but still it will be one day and not another,
it will be like switching on the light
in the night train, you will never
see through the reflection again.

And here it is. Wherever you go,
you will find yourself
already there—sitting
not in the centre, but at the end of the bench,
beneath the eaves, bag clutched in your lap.
The rain comes in sideways,
and your trouser cuffs are wet:
the dots have joined like ink.
It's unmistakeably you,
the way, having slept against the headrest,
curled around the bag,
your hair now stands up at the crown,
fronds of bedraggled fern,
the way your trousers bunch in the flex of the hip.
You must have alighted hours ago,
and when the light behind the clouds
went down beneath the chain link fence,
when asked—Are you alright?
You must have said—
I'm waiting for someone
to collect me. You're too polite to say—
no.

Siren

Out on the balcony, where the air moves
and the sky flows in over the rooftops,
there may be something better than this, some place
the spine is not locked like a puzzle, where
that old, swallowed burr beneath the ribs
could dislodge.

In here you are always reading
too many things at once, rancorous,
so that later, nothing may be felt
but a diffuse discontent.
You are late for an appointment
for a purpose you've forgotten
in a place you have no map for.
You are doing everything faster
and faster. When things fall down,
you kick them aside.

But you cannot just slip outside
and take an updraft to the sky.
There is an intermediate stage,
which you cannot bear. The bounds
        of the body itself,
which contains the burr that was swallowed,
                will need to dissolve.
Ha, no, you are making this up!
        The truth is, you do not know
what it is, though sometimes
you think you hear a dim whirl of sound
like a siren, or a child's voice calling
from its guessed, general direction. But
you just don't know. You don't know
anything.

Unless

The ants are in the kitchen again,
the bin smells, the cornices rot,
the garden is dying. Somewhere
the omphalos waits for me.
I am sure this key I have opens
the secret vault; I must try it
in all locks. The field of locks to try
stretches to the horizon;
it covers the earth. But one day
       there will be a star
among stars in the dark sky, and I will know it,
it will be the one I have waited for.
Is there not something
that is coming for me? A card
in the deck of the days of a life,
       which is dealt
and dealt.
The milk sours; animals hate me.
Is it here, beneath this
unwashed plate? In this
furled sock? In the place,
already checked, where a car key
may be found, but not
till much later,
party started, train
       missed?

Consolation and its discontents

What is the peculiar
            consolation of a sky
like a violet lamp
above a crunched-foil sea?
Meanwhile, your mother
does not love you.
Still, there are the black
strokes of the trees
and the toy car lights
            on the rim of the bay.
In the sand, an eagle has lain down
and died, feather bunting
on a barn of bones,
wings still outstretched, as if
life ended
            still in flight.

Return

I dreamed I caught a sky-blue bird
in a cloud of silk scarf,
in the waxed burlap dark
beneath my childhood bed.
Tiny wings pulsed, bones
like toothpicks; did I hold it
too tight, or not tight enough?
We argued at the door—
you had installed some medieval lock
and had to let me out. It was just like the time
I got my ears pierced, which was just
like the time I came back from camp
with the wrong look on my face.

On the grass, the bird was still, and
we craned like people on the edge
of a precipice. Then
it took wing and was gone,
to a stand of eucalypts
tall as a building—the flats
next door had disappeared.
Other, bright birds were whirling and diving.
You said, full of wonder—I'm afraid
they'll fall out of the sky. I want
so much to say the bird is me. But it
flew away, and you and I
went back in the house together.

The note from God

One night I came home and
there was a note on the kitchen table
from God. I knew it had to be him
because I live alone, and the cleaner
was not due till next week. It was the same
cheery sort of note the cleaner leaves, and
he, too, had not realised my novelty pen
that looks like a stick
is actually a pen, not a stick, and had thought he had to write
with the green ink from the four-colour pen
in which all the other inks have run out
(you could see on the corner of the pad
he had tested the blue and black first).
The note said,
> Hi, it's me.
> The light on the landing's out.
> It's me who keeps leaving those dishes in the sink overnight.
> Sorry about that thing with your stepdad.
> Okay, I think that's everything.
> —G

So that was that.

At first I admit I struggled
that he just called it
that thing with your stepdad.

Later I tried to decide
if anything had changed.
Was the tower of livid storm front
rolling in across the bay
more lovely than it would have been before?
More terrible?

To be sure, there were still
just as many dishes in the sink.

The woman from the real estate
never called me back, so in the end I just
got on the ladder
and changed the bulb myself, supposing
I did not really need her,
or God, or anyone
for that one.

Afterword

A poem is a way of saying something that can't be said in any more straightforward way—or ought to be—so to be asked to explain my poems makes me fear I must have failed at saying those somethings I was trying to say. Another objection is that explaining risks undercutting the way the poems work. They are impressionistic, using compressed gestures to suggest a larger subject. The reader makes an empathetic leap to fill in the details, employing the materials of their own life experience and internal affective landscape to create a melange of meaning that will necessarily feel more urgent, more true than any direct account from me of the poem's 'facts' ever could. If I explain, I repudiate this empathetic melange, demanding it be discarded in favour of something much thinner, less energised.

This is to say, I came very close to dedicating this volume to my mother, but on balance I thought the poems had said enough.

Notes

'Mum, again': I'm afraid the phrase 'softened... almost to melody' is from H G Wells's *The War of the Worlds*, via Jeff Wayne's 1978 musical adaptation with which I was obsessed as a child. I have tried to get rid of it, but I just like it too much.

Acknowledgements

The poems in this volume span more than ten years by publication date, probably more than fifteen by date of first composition. There are far too many people to thank, and many of them may not even remember me. For feedback I thank again Lisa Jacobson, Andy Jackson, Terry Jaensch, Brook Emery and everyone in associated workshops, and Joan Houlihan and everyone at Colrain in New Mexico in 2015. I am also delighted once more to acknowledge Bundanon Trust for the assistance of a residency in 2014, where I alarmed and was alarmed by the cows that feature in 'Exile', and was thoroughly rumbled by the famous sub-floor wombats. Finally, thanks to family and friends who continue to commit the act of reading poems merely because I wrote them. You fools.

A number of poems in this collection appeared previously in the chapbook, *The Things the Mind Sees Happen*, Puncher & Wattmann, 2019. Individual poems have also appeared (sometimes in an earlier version), to my great pleasure, in Australia in *Meanjin, Island, Westerly, Australian Book Review, Cordite Poetry Review, Best Australian Poems 2012, The Adas 2015* (prize anthology), *The Seagull Poetry Prize 2009* (anthology), *foam:e, Hecate* and *Eureka Street*; and overseas in *Barrow Street 4 x 2, Antipodes, Orbis, Oxford Poetry*, the *Montreal International Poetry Prize Long List Anthology 2013* and *The London Magazine*.

About the author

Belinda Rule's chapbook, *The Things the Mind Sees Happen*, was commended in the Anne Elder Award 2019. *Hyperbole* is her first full-length collection. She lives in Melbourne, where she has been a history academic and a university administrator, and now works for a medical college. Her work has appeared widely in Australia, the UK and the US over many years.

www.ingramcontent.com/pod-product-compliance
Ingram Content Group Australia Pty Ltd
76 Discovery Rd, Dandenong South VIC 3175, AU
AUHW020841060325
407965AU00004B/54

9 780645 009033